UNCLOGGED

Targeting the Top 10 Mindset Cloggers to Business Success

MONIQUE DOUGLAS

SPARK Publications
Charlotte, North Carolina

*Unclogged: Targeting the Top 10
Mindset Cloggers to Business Success*
Monique Douglas

Visit CBKBrandingandConsulting.com to contact the author for speaking or training engagements.

Designed, produced, and published by SPARK Publications
SPARKpublications.com
Charlotte, North Carolina

Photography by Kevin Douglas
www.CBKBrandingandConsulting.com

Stock Images: 80708184 / GettyImages

Softcover, full color, April 2022,
ISBN: 978-1-953555-27-4

Library of Congress Control Number: 2022904180

In Memory of Kimyon Zari

(June 20, 1961 ◈ December 26, 2021)

This Diamond was a close friend, client
& contributor to this published work.
Her untimely death preceded its completion.

DEDICATION

This book is dedicated to my parents, Christopher and Stephanie Stubbs. Without their insistence on the importance of good communication (both verbal and written), I would not have such a beautiful ability to transfer powerful messages into the hands and hearts of others.

Next would be my four children: Gordon, Monet, Chloe, and Victoria who have all been such a wonderful support of my entrepreneurial endeavors over their years of growing up.

To my granddaughter Maddie, who passed away in March 2018, for being the inspiration for me to complete this book. During the short time that we had to celebrate her life, she and her parents, Monet and Brandon, taught us all that tomorrow is not promised, so we must make every moment count. We cannot afford to put aside for tomorrow what we can do today.

Next, I dedicate this published work to the hundreds of individuals I have had the opportunity to train, coach, mentor, and lead over the span of thirty years in my professional career. Working with them has provided me with such a wealth of insight that I felt it was time to take some of the key components I have derived from working with them and pen them. Of course, they cannot all be mentioned. I have mentioned a few whom I have coached, mentored, or had meaningful conversations with that are much closer than the rest. While they may not be high-ranking officials or have celebrity status according to this world's standards, they are more than that to me; they reflect the reality of everyday unsung professionals working through real-life scenarios to achieve business success, and I am ecstatic to highlight their achievements. Here are eleven of them you will be introduced to throughout the book, and I know you will enjoy their contributions: Mike Knoble, Melissa Baker, Kimyon Zari, Rita Garnto, Shell Richardson, Nesha Pai, Kevin Douglas, Audra Hill, LaGuida Moore, Francine Marie, and Nora Richardson.

FOREWORD

There are so many times as professionals where we set goals for ourselves but are not able to move forward in achieving them. For some reason, unbeknownst to ourselves, we are just plain stuck! We experience a feeling of being "clogged up," and it's not a pretty state to be in. Getting "unclogged" can feel like a daunting process.

A clear mind can cause mountains to be built, climbed, and/or moved. When we understand the power of our minds, we will have the ability to move from where we are to where we deserve to be. Remember that, as Napoleon Hill so eloquently stated in *Think and Grow Rich*[1], "our only limitations are those we set up in our own minds."

Upon reading this book, you will realize that many of the things that cause us to be stuck are not always business related; however, not addressing certain "mindset cloggers" even in our personal lives can contribute to an inability to focus on business goals. This book is designed to help professionals identify the area that has them stagnant (Examine the Stoppage), deal with it head on (Plunge It), develop clarity of mind (Flush It), and then move forward toward business success (Enjoy the Clear Passage).

May you find the clarity needed to propel you to the next level in your professional journey, and may

---

1. Napoleon Hill, *Think and Grow Rich* (The Ralston Society, 1937).

you share this book with others who you know can benefit from it. Denzel Washington said it best in his book *A Hand to Guide Me*[2], "At the end of the day it's not about what you have or even what you've accomplished. ... It's about who you've lifted up, who you've made better. It's about what you've given back." In other words, part of our professional success is empowering and servicing others to achieve their goals as well.

Are you ready? Let's get *Unclogged*!

Monique

---

2. Denzel Washington, *A Hand to Guide Me* (Meredith Books, 2006).

CONTENTS

INTRODUCTION

Getting clogged and then unclogged is not a onetime occurrence. For example, as I began to write my story so that I could share it with you I realized I've been clogged so many times in my life, and yet I made it through and learned so many lessons along the way. I then decided the best way to tell my story and explain to you why I am able to help you identify, plunge, and flush so many of your mindset cloggers is because I've overcome so many within my own journey. So here it goes: my journey to getting *Unclogged*.

Clogged as a Newlywed

I married young at twenty-one-years old. I came from a religious family where marriage was very serious and sacred. My husband was my first everything. Within our first year of marriage, I began to see habits in his behavior that I was not accustomed to, from the only man I had to hold his behavior up to—my father. His behaviors began to get worse and although I was not happy, I put up with them because I assumed I just had to. After all, that is what my vow said, 'till death do us part,' right?!

Lesson Learned: What you may have seen all of your life as normal does not always transfer to your life's situation. As badly as you may wish it to be so, every relationship will have its own unique characteristics, and you must be willing to call it for what it is. Pretending will not improve the situation.

Clogged as a New Mother

We had our first child four years later. We had a picture-perfect life as a young couple. We both had great jobs, we bought a home, we drove nice cars, we were stylish, and we seemed to have it all in order. Then six months after giving birth to child number one, I found out I was pregnant with number two! Screech and Halt! That would clog anyone up! This was going to be like having twins!

How would I juggle this? What about childcare for two small infants? Is it worth me even working my corporate job? Oh goodness … would that mean I would lose my identity if I had to become a stay-at-home mom?

Oh, and by the way, my husband's habits were not improving. I was becoming filled with anxiety while trying to juggle the infants and pretend as a "good wife" that I was happy. All because I perceived expectations from others around me that I was trying to live up to.

Lesson Learned: We put unnecessary pressure on ourselves trying to live up to other's expectations. Many times, the individuals pressuring you to meet their standards of perfection are among the most flawed in their own relationships.

Clogged as a New Mother in Corporate

As so many women struggle with, I too had to contend with the decision of adjusting my career choice in order to care for my children affordably. Oh yes, let me not forget to mention as soon as I potty trained child number two, I found out I was pregnant with number three. What type of work could I possibly do from home with three small children? Was I even cut out to be at home all day with little ones? Were all of my dreams to be successful in corporate going to be shot? Stuck once again! I worked in a call center. I had worked my way to a senior representative and a training assistant after a short time on the job and loved it all. Until the day they came to me asking me to move to a desk closer to the restrooms so my frequent trips to the restroom as a result of my pregnancy would take up less time when I unplugged from the phone systems. They said I was negatively affecting the call center's stats.

My response: "What! You are monitoring how much I pee?" A week later, I provided them a two weeks' notice of my resignation.

Lesson Learned: I am not a robot! Therefore, I do not have to accept treatment as if I am. I can create my own options.

Clogged as a New Mother with Babies & Entrepreneurship

Our solution to creating revenue at home with three small ones was to open a licensed family home daycare. This was my first entrepreneurial endeavor. I quickly learned I loved the children but dealing with the parents was the stress factor (not making payments on time, picking up their children when they wanted to, and accusing us of not doing things that as parents was their responsibility). To this day, I have incredible respect for anyone who works in this industry. I shifted industries and moved into another home-based business centered around direct sales in cosmetics.

I was able to have more flexibility working around my children, I had tons more fun, had a successful twenty-year career making executive level income, experienced high-level trainings, had international travel opportunities, and the pleasure of grooming hundreds of women in business along the way.

Lesson Learned: Your journey may not always go in the path you set out for yourself. Detours may occur, and you must be open to them; for they may lead you to a path better suited for your current situation.

Clogged Going through Separation & Divorce Number One

Speaking of shifts in life's journey...things were not moving in the right direction at home. I was so full of stress and anxiety I dropped to 115 lbs., ended up having anxiety attacks, and I got on meds for stress and anxiety. The physical, mental, and emotional toll on me forced me to make a difficult decision. After fifteen years of marriage and three small children, I walked out. My mind was clogged and cluttered with fear. (I had never lived on my own let alone with three children.) Was I a failure for having a failed marriage? Where would I obtain funds to start all over? I also wondered how others would view me for leaving a situation even though they had no clue how long, and the depth, of all I had experienced.

Lesson Learned: My journey is my journey! I do not need to wait on validation from others. I've learned to walk it out in the best way I know how. Seek counsel but realize you must still put in the work to survive your personal journey. The path may not be easy, but you have been designed with the creativity and stamina to make it through. What did I do? I withdrew my 401(k) to get a fresh start for myself and my children. Yes, I started fresh. And yes, we had a month with no gas and electricity, but we survived! I've had monthly eviction notices on my door and have gone to church pantries to get groceries for my household. I've been denied temporary assistance from the government, and I'm a taxpayer. I had no food or no idea where my next source of income would come from. Determination, seeking counsel from those more experienced, humility, and tenacity has helped my growth each step of the way!

Lesson Learned: You cannot give up! It's not an option. You are not your circumstances. They are just steppingstones to prepare you and stretch you for what is in store.

Clogged as a Single Mom of Three Young Ones & Entrepreneurship

In the first year of my separation, I was given a whopping $24 by my children's father, and it was placed under a doormat for me to pick up. It was that day that I learned humiliation. I learned "if it's gonna be, it will be up to me." I knew that I would have to remain an entrepreneur in order to have the flexibility in my schedule to work with my children. So I focused on building my cosmetic sales business to a point where I could sustain myself and my children on entrepreneurial endeavors. I could take them and pick them up from school and avoid paying childcare expenses that I certainly could not afford at the time.

Yes, there were days I was in tears because things weren't easy. Yes, I felt like I was not rock bottom but under the rock. Yes, I was angry when, in the midst of me working hard to just survive, I was pulled into court to fight for the right to have joint custody of my three children when "he" tried to prove I was an unfit parent and wanted to obtain full custody to avoid paying me child support. Yes, I was "clogged up" and swirling with emotions! But this I knew: I had to figure it out and keep moving forward. Claims of my unfit parenthood were proven false, and I obtained joint custody. Then later, I was able to obtain full physical custody. I stayed focused on my business and continued to grow and sustain myself and the kids, and found ways to keep joy flowing in our humble home.

Lesson Learned: The journey to success is not easy. It's filled with hills and valleys, times of plenty and times of famine. You must, however, keep bringing water to the desert land, and it will reap fruit in due time.

Clogged as I Entered Marriage Number Two with Three Preteens

I decided to give marriage another chance. I, however, was unprepared for the dynamics of bringing someone into a home with three preteens. Especially since he had never lived with his own children as they grew up. More adjustments, more stoppages, and more things to figure out!

Lesson Learned: Flexibility is key. Never underestimate your ability to shift. But stay wide awake too.

Clogged as a Forty-year-old Finding Out She Is Pregnant with Child Number Four

"What!!!" That was my response after having a miscarriage three months prior when I was told "you are pregnant"! My dad said, "Why are you surprised? Haven't you figured out yet how that happens?" Well yes, but that doesn't lessen the shock factor. The fear of losing another child. The reality of my age (let alone that of my husband who was nine years older than me). Plus, the HUGE elephant in the room was that we were in an unhealthy relationship bearing a child. Once again, we had to figure it out. And we did, despite gestational diabetes and a premature birth.

Lesson Learned: "God has a sense of humor" some say. I believe that to be so because I would have never dreamed at my age that this would happen. We made the best of the unexpected and rolled with it!

Clogged Going through Separation & Divorce Number Two with a Young Child Still at Home

Yes, we had our beautiful bundle. We went through a drug relapse and a twelve-year roller coaster of instability. I went back on meds twice as a result of my stress and anxiety being re-ignited. I could have never predicted I would be "clogged up" again. What I knew was for my own welfare and that of my children, I had to exit another toxic situation.

Lesson Learned: Pay attention to all of the details before you make relationship decisions. Understand that relationships are not just for you if your children are involved. You cannot sacrifice your health and wellbeing for toxic situations. Loving someone who is special to you may mean removing yourself from the equation, so that they can work through and focus on their own challenges.

Clogged Experiencing the Death of My Granddaughter

In all that I have been through in my life, I thought there was really nothing else that could rock my core. However, the loss of a loved one, my granddaughter, brought me to a level of grief I could not imagine. While working a job I was really enjoying, living in the area I always wanted to, and seeing my children finally settle into their own, we were presented with news we were unprepared for.

Results from normal testing within my daughter's pregnancy in her first trimester came back that her baby had a chromosomal disorder known as Trisomy 18. A rare disorder in which most youth do not live past one year. My daughter and her husband decided to continue with the pregnancy despite the diagnosis and our beautiful granddaughter was born. She was a picture of beauty.

Shortly after birth, we learned she had two holes in her heart and a malfunctioning liver, which eventually ended up in her system being poisoned. Our sweet Maddie was such a fighter; she had a will to live and was a spitfire. She touched the lives of nurses, doctors, and all of our family members and friends who had an opportunity to interact with her. Her beautiful eyes drew us all in, always reassuring us she would be OK. She took her last breath in my arms at two-and-a-half-months old. Watching the strength of her parents as they held her until every ounce of life force left her body was touching but sobering. The journey of grief was for me a long one. It took me a year to stop crying incessantly at the thought of my daughter and her husband's loss. To see my child experience that level of pain was heart wrenching. I was clogged mentally and emotionally. At times I just felt foggy and lacked energy and motivation to move forward. Through prayer and lots of self-talk, I worked my way through my period of grieving and began to revisit all that is important in life and business. I began re-establishing goals and getting unclogged.

Lesson Learned: Even life's most devastating moments can become tests to your endurance. Even our beautiful Maddie left lessons for us, such as "enjoy every moment for tomorrow is not promised"; "worrying about what you cannot change in life will keep you stopped up, so learn how to release that anxiety, and focus on what you have the ability to control"; "grief is a natural response to the trauma of death; you do not have to apologize for going through it. No one can tell you how long it should take you to go through it; and yes, you can work through it."

Clogged Working at a Job That Does Not Appreciate My Value

A year after working through the emotions of the loss of my granddaughter, I began to experience a battle on the job I loved that side-swiped me. I was working ungodly hours to ensure we maintained a standard of excellence but was working with another manager who did not share the same standard. I witnessed behavior on the job with both staff and clients that compromised all that I was working hard to maintain. It seemed like we would move a few steps forward but then fall triple the number of steps backward. We couldn't maintain staff because no one could deal with this individual's lack of professionalism. Clients I worked so hard to obtain were leaving due to ill treatment; and whenever eyes were glaring at this individual from upper management, they would deflect to me resulting in my value being questioned. After several instances of ill treatment and disrespect, I made one of the most difficult decisions in my career: I walked out the door and never looked back.

Lesson Learned: You must know your value. We are so accustomed to allowing others to dictate and manipulate us based on what they want us to believe our value is in order to fit into their ulterior motives. Most of the time, we succumb out of the fear that we may never find a situation to work in where we are respected and paid according to our true value. I have learned that by allowing others to devalue you, you will stay clogged up, unhappy, and feeling a lack of self-worth. It takes faith to know that you do not need to compromise on your value to make others feel better. In the long run, you will be stripped of your joy. Find what is for you … it's out there!

Clogged Entering Marriage Number Three and Opening a Brick and Mortar in the Middle of a Pandemic

What I failed to mention was that, in the midst of losing my granddaughter and dealing with drama on the job, I was also wrapping up a divorce from husband number two. So just when I thought I had enough, was exhausted emotionally, and clogged to the brim, I was sent someone who changed the trajectory of my journey. After a number of years, our relationship moved from a friendship to a relationship that ended in marriage in the middle of the COVID-19 pandemic of 2020.

We also took a huge step by opening a brick-and-mortar location six weeks before the pandemic. We opened and then had to close when we were mandated by the state to "shelter in place" as a result of the pandemic. We were "clogged up" as we sat at home asking ourselves, "Had we made the right decision? Where would we go from here? How will we survive?"

To "stop up" things some more the following week, we each lost every contract we had secured for the year.

Just like that ... income flew out the door. I remember the pause. I think for two weeks we could barely talk. We both became introspective, and we knew we needed to come up with a plan—quickly.

The beautiful part was that, together, we did; we became innovative in our programming and marketing of our brand, we came up with "micro" event concepts, we applied for grant opportunities, and we sought support from community partners and organizations put in place to assist small businesses. We survived, used our location to bless many others struggling as well, and are so grateful we are still standing.

Lesson Learned: A business coach once said to me: "It's OK to have a pity party for twenty-four hours, but after that you've got to get up and get moving!" That has always stayed in my head. Life will continue to throw curve balls, but you cannot continue to lie down and wallow in pity. You must get up or you never will; however, it really is your choice.

My children, my community partners, my husband, and those who I have coached over the years have always said the biggest thing they admire about me is my resilience. I am always transparent, and I am not afraid to show who I am authentically. I have grown to love the woman I am with all of my flaws, my scrapes, and my bruises from my own life's journey. It is with such joy that I have chosen to share them with you. *Unclogged* is designed to truly help you identify what is holding you back from your business success, understand you are not alone as we all face various challenges, and have the confidence to know you can overcome and move onto the success you desire.

MINDSET CLOGGER #1

YOU

Greatness is within you. It may be buried deep, but make no doubt about it. . .you've got it!

Examine the Stoppage

Are you surprised that I came out of the gate addressing you? Well, don't be. Most of the time, it is our own mindset that sets us back from moving forward in our businesses. Over the years I have coached men and women in a variety of industries and a variety of professional levels, and it has been clear to me that there is one thing they all share in common when they are seeking direction: a need to adjust their own perspectives in a certain category of their personal or business life.

Plunge It

There is no way around the fact that your business success must begin with your personal attitude. It's so much easier to blame others when things are not going the way you desire. You must condition your mind to understand that while others or unforeseen circumstances may have contributed to your discomfort, loss of business, or stress factors, it is ultimately you and only you that can turn around the trajectory of your personal or professional life.

Developing a reverse mentality is a must! Here are a few tips to help you plunge this disposition so that your mind will be open for the success you deserve.

Try a Fresh Perspective

Sometimes you need to perk up or try a new twist or spin on what you do. Make it fun and exciting for you and your team to promote, and watch how your enthusiasm wakes up you, your team, and your clients too! Get creative and out of your daily routine of business and watch how business will become more interesting.

Be Prepared to Work

The reality that success takes effort is not always what we want to hear. If you are determined to be successful, you must adjust your mindset to realize work is required. Sometimes the work may not be what we would like to do, but success may require your involvement in aspects of the job that may not always be your favorite. You must have an all-hands-on-deck-including-me mentality until you are able to delegate what you don't desire to do.

Put Pen to Paper

One of the most difficult tasks, once you realize the hang-up is you, is writing an action plan to hold yourself accountable. By doing so, you have a point of reference as to the steps you must take to reach your goals. You also can no longer blame anyone else but yourself when action items are not completed. Even more effective would be setting a date by which each task must be completed. Make it real by committing in ink to a time frame to get it done. Just imagine, if you don't complete the goal by that date, you are sure to be a whole lot further from your professional success.

Flush It

You will notice that this section in every chapter will be the same. It will begin with a positive affirmation to allow you to let go of this particular mindset clogger, and then it will present a series of exercises for you to complete in order to work through your thoughts and hold yourself accountable to move forward.

No longer will I be bound to this mindset clogger, for it increases my anxiety and decreases my productivity! It is holding me back from my professional success. I am now free and walking with clarity because I have released it and flushed it down the drain! I am now unclogged!

Contemplate It

Let's complete your "flushing" by completing the following exercise.

Record five areas where you realize you can change your professional perspective:

1

____

2

____

3

____

4

____

5

____

Keeping these perspectives in mind, provide an overview of how you will implement these changes and then put a date of completion on each. (Remember: "a goal without a date is simply a dream.")

1
____

2
____

3
____

4
____

5
____

Interview with

Melissa Baker

Director of Education
Merle Norman Cosmetics

Tell us a little about your career background.

I've had an incredible, unintended thirty-year career in the cosmetics industry. I feel so fortunate to have fallen into something I have an innate love and talent for that touches women's lives through the work that I get to do. I've made a life and am living from it. My experience includes retail sales, events, marketing, and education for top beauty brands in the industry. It's taken me all over the country and internationally. I'm now leveraging that expertise in a new way to modernize branding, merchandising, and learning for a legacy cosmetics brand.

When you evaluate your professional journey, what would you identify as your greatest mindset clogger?

My greatest mindset clogger was me! Looking back, my mindset (how much I believed in myself or not) was relative to where I was in my career and level of success. I've achieved a lot, but I couldn't always see what I had achieved and the abilities that got me there.

What did you do to overcome it?

Circumstances gave me the opportunity to bet on myself and take a hiatus from the comfort of being employed by a company to leaping into the unknown and unsecured ride of entrepreneurism. I was elated, but fear set in, and I was paralyzed. I serendipitously met Monique and invested in myself with a one-on-one coaching session. I was used to being that coach for other people; even the best athletes have a coach.

What advice would you give to those struggling in this area?

Be excited when you figure out that you are what's standing in the way. You only have control over you and your thoughts anyway, so you can get to work on it anytime. I knew that I was at a place where I needed someone else who could see my talents and reflect back to me. A book wasn't going to do it this time. I needed to level up what I was doing, and that was with a coach.

What successes have you achieved as a direct result of plunging this clogger?

Monique helped me to see that my successes weren't a stroke of luck. I had the talent and had put in the skills to achieve my success. That was a mindset shift that allowed me to do things I had only dreamed of before. Some of the "immediate" effects were that I coauthored a book, ran my own business, and became a recognized leader in my community and a sought-after peer for fellow entrepreneurs. This opened me up to continue taking larger leaps, like a cross-country move, and taking on new roles in my career currently while still looking to the future and asking, "What else can I do?"

Connect with Melissa: mjbgrace@mjbinc.net

Enjoy the Clear Passage

With a freed-up mind, you can begin the process of progression! Wasting your mind is counterproductive. Allowing yourself to be free of self-induced restraints will open your mind to endless possibilities in your field.

"My greatest mindset clogger was *me!* Looking back, my mindset (how much I believed in myself or not) was relative to where I was in my career and level of success."

MINDSET CLOGGER #2

Seeds Planted from Your Past

You must rip up and clear out the weeds of negativity from your past that are choking you, in order to bloom to your fullest potential.

Examine the Stoppage

This topic is so deep because it goes far beyond business activities. You may not remotely realize that you are clogged up as a result of previous life experiences and influences. People or experiences in our life journeys can have damaging effects on our ability to reach our professional goals. Until you face these "rotten seeds," they will continue to bloom at unexpected times in your life and, like weeds, can choke out your creativity, productivity, and ability to succeed. Let's examine some of the influences that can block us up.

Trauma

It has been shared by medical experts that trauma in life, whether as a youth or an adult, can have long-term effects. The difficult part about physical, emotional, or mental abuse is that an individual may appear recovered outwardly; however, triggers may result in reliving these events in their minds repeatedly throughout life.

So how can this affect your professional success? Let's provide an example. You may be coasting along in your place of employment, achieving recognition for your amazing talents, and excelling to a point where you are now ready for a promotion. You then encounter an individual in a role of leadership whom you will eventually report to. They may communicate verbally or through body language something inappropriate that may flash you back to a moment in your life that you have been suppressing or thought you had gotten beyond. Suddenly, you become immobilized. You lose your zeal to move forward at your job. Fears set in, and you don't even want to show up to work the next day. You are clogged up.

Playback of Negative Talk from Influencers in Your Past

You may not have grown up in a nurturing environment. Maybe your parent, guardian, or influencer in your life did not provide positive messages. You may have constantly been made to feel you were not worthy to succeed. You were not fed affirmations that inspired you to be your best. You may instead have been fed a mental diet of inadequacy, negativity, and were stripped of self-worth—constantly told you were stupid, ugly, dumb, fat, and that you would never amount to anything. Being fed this type of mental abuse can again be very damaging in your adult life. The mind becomes a tape recorder of sorts. When you seem to be at your peak and you are feeling well accomplished, your mind can begin to play back these negative messages, and you can easily become entrapped once again by feelings of fear and inadequacy. You may begin to "dumb down" your abilities because you feel you are not worthy of the attention you receive. You may feel frozen and no longer want to pursue the next level in your career because of the negative self-talk playing back in your head. You feel clogged up.

Pressures from Those Who Don't Want to See You Succeed

It's amazing how our circles can impact our ability to succeed. Believe it or not, you will have individuals in both your personal and professional circles who just can't stand to see you move up. Instead of rejoicing in your progress, they will look for ways to discourage you from moving up. For some, it may not be malicious; it may just come from their own personal insecurities. Nonetheless, it can severely impact your mindset if you are not careful. With others, they intentionally try to sabotage your success. They may gossip about you, plant seeds of doubt in others' minds regarding your abilities or may be bold enough to tell you to your face they don't believe in you and feel you should not pursue progression. This can be among the most devastating because you may feel betrayed since this is coming from those you felt you could look up to and confide in. You feel clogged up.

Plunge It

It's so easy for others to say, "Just get over it," or "That was in your past; why are you even focusing on it?" or "Why are you even attempting? You aren't ready for that!" I'm here to tell you that reasoning is foolish, and you cannot afford to give it ear. It will keep you stuck in a rut.

Release the past as best you can. Use what is at your disposal to do so. There is nothing wrong with seeking the help of medical professionals if balancing the impact from early life trauma is affecting you.

You may need to confront those whose negative talk is impacting you and let them know that you will no longer give ear to their damaging talk. You can emphasize that from this day forward, you choose to associate with and allow your mind to be fed from the energies of those who inspire you and are in positions where you want to be. Unless they choose to positively impact your growth, you must choose to love them from afar until they have a mindset change and can support your efforts rather than tear them down.

Colleagues who want to see you step back—perhaps because they want the same promotion you're working toward—need to be dealt with the same way. Their poor disposition is usually a clear indicator of why you are being looked at for the position and not them. Don't allow yourself to be bullied! Know your worth and work in harmony with it. A bully can't continue if you refuse to play the game. Don't feed into their mindset. Purge and plunge their disposition out and stay focused on your goals!

Flush It

Repeat your positive affirmation and complete the following exercise.

No longer will I be bound to this mind clogger, for it increases my anxiety and decreases my productivity! It is holding me back from my professional success. I am now free and walking with clarity because I have released it and flushed it down the drain! I am now unclogged.

Contemplate It

Let's complete your "flushing" by completing the following exercise.

Write the greatest negative seed planted in your mind from your past and then write the full name of the person that fed it to you. Take a red marker and cross it out completely with a huge X. The red is symbolic of the expression STOP, and while you are putting the huge X over it and them, repeat to yourself your affirmation above. Let it go!

Kimyon Zari

Diamond Coach
Speaker and Facilitator

Tell us a little about your career background.

I am the daughter of Barbara Lewis and Grover Williams. I blessed the city of Springfield, Massachusetts—home of the Basketball Hall of Fame and Merriam-Webster's Dictionary—on Tuesday, June 20, 1961. Although both of my parents were born and raised in North Carolina, they met in Washington, DC, while seeking job opportunities and decided to date. A sudden family crisis brought my mother to Springfield, Massachusetts, with me in tow, and this is where she called home. Living in Reed Village Projects laid a foundation for growth or setbacks. Reed housed over one hundred single moms with children according to their individual needs. This environment could be considered a breeding ground for comfort because the perks were set up for women to remain there long term. We knew our neighbors, and we knew the rules of this space. However, if we stayed too long, we would begin to talk, walk, and act like everyone in this space. Fortunately, my mother had one dream for us. She wanted to buy a house with a backyard to call our own.

When you evaluate your professional journey, what would you identify as your greatest mindset clogger?

"Don't you dare think outside the box or try to create a better life." Since everyone else followed the crowd, I found myself in and out of line with the same crew, doing the same things more times than I can count. Although it had occurred to me that I could also create my own backyard, I knew climbing this mountain would be challenging based on my upbringing to "be seen and not heard." I didn't know that I had the wherewithal to start projects I dreamed about, nor did I think that I knew where to really begin. However, over the years, my perspective and understanding of life shifted when I decided to leave the environment that molded me.

What did you do to overcome it?

What I know for sure is that different cloggers revealed themselves at different levels and times. In July 1997, I attended Maria Dowd's African American Women on Tour (AAWOT) event in Chicago. I chose to attend the women's retreat instead of the main conference, and it was a treat! I learned the value of my name and why it was important. The facilitator discussed how to recognize the value of our worth through self-assessments and self-awareness. Additionally, she encouraged self-knowledge because it is essential to our growth and development through decision-making. At the end of three days, I was armed with a checklist of ten decisions to handle, manage, or eliminate when I returned home. I was so intrigued that I changed my first name immediately to match the feeling in my heart. I prayed about it, and five years later, I changed my name legally. It was the beginning.

What advice would you give to those struggling in this area?

If I learned anything of value moving through this life, here it is: use your struggle(s) to upgrade your life. In my case, uncertainty, fear, doubt, unhealthy relationships, and lack of self-awareness all played a role in the messes I created when guarding my heart would have been the result of clear communication with myself. But I guess experiencing icky situations to exercise my mental wings was necessary in order to learn how to power up. Nonetheless, I used every struggle to land right back on my feet. Create a set of values and principles to stand on for leverage. Seek assistance in managing your overall health and wellness, which is critical to living well. I'm still a work in progress.

What successes have you achieved as a direct result of plunging this clogger?

Success is different for everyone, and I have had many [successes], from power auditions to performing for presidents across the waters and realizing a billboard charting single, "Fantasize," which is still played around the world. I interviewed highly successful business executives, writers, and celebrities, including many featured in *Black Enterprise* magazine, who shared their trials and victories to success and the issues they encountered along their respective journeys. I have endured not one but two major heart surgeries, and I'm here to tell it. The only success that really matters to me is that I embrace my whole self, and I have my children to thank for paving the way. My philosophy is simple: appreciate the value of your whole life no matter how it turns out, and then walk gently on the earth. Namaste.

I think Wynton Marsalis says it best: "Each moment is a procession from the future into the past and the sweet spot is always the present. Live in that sweet spot. Be present."

Enjoy the Clear Passage

When you are attempting to leap to new levels, you cannot afford to allow others to cause you to stop dead in your tracks. More importantly, you cannot stay frozen in time. You must address the issues at hand either directly with the individuals or through resources available to you. At times, the issue may be serious enough for you to seek medical assistance from an expert. It may be a concern that is of large enough magnitude on your job to address your HR department, or some matters may require a legal professional to handle them. The key to clarity of mind is to not allow these matters to linger. Handle them swiftly and through the appropriate channels and enjoy a peace of mind that is necessary for you to experience your next level of success.

"If I learned anything of value
moving through this life, here
it is: use your struggle(s)
to upgrade your life."

MINDSET CLOGGER #3

Lack of Confidence

Watch out world, because when you step into your fullest potential, you will be EPIC.

Examine the Stoppage

You may be wondering how you know if this is the area where you're clogged. Do you find yourself second-guessing your abilities? Do you get a sick feeling in your stomach when asked to handle an assignment that you are not accustomed to doing? Do you engage in creative avoidance when you know there is an activity you must complete, but it requires you to approach others that are in positions higher than yours? Do you enter a room of professionals and try to find an excuse for why you must leave early because being there makes you nervous at the thought of having to meet someone you don't know? These may all be signs of a lack of confidence. It is important to work on this matter because, if allowed to fester, it can paralyze your success. The first thing you must know is that you are not alone. Therefore, lack of confidence is toward the top of my top 10 list. If you've identified this as an area you need to work on, let's get to the business of working on this obstacle to your professional success!

Low Self-Esteem

This is really the greatest reason for a lack of confidence. The way that you feel about yourself really does affect the things you think about, the way you behave, the way you treat and react to others, and ultimately how successful you will be in life.

Negative feedback or situations undermine your self-esteem, and that can continue to affect your performance and success every day. A negative comment from a boss or coworker can unlock some deep-seated fear, triggering a limiting belief that can change your entire outlook and create a new filter through which you view your abilities in your life or career.

Plunge It

If you are suffering from lack of confidence because of low self-esteem in your professional life, here are a few reminders to keep you grounded and help you reverse this clogger and plunge it.

Remember that you are not perfect, and you will make mistakes.

A common mistake of those suffering from lack of confidence is the feeling that they must prove they are perfect. This is so far from the truth. In fact, no matter how successful a person appears, they have made mistakes in the past and will make mistakes in the future. That's just a part of the growth process. No need to beat yourself up about something you cannot change. You will make mistakes because you are human. With that in mind, the more important factor is whether you are learning lessons from your mistakes and using them to make you better.

You can ask questions, listen, and respond in an objective way.

For some reason, many professionals are afraid to ask questions. They feel that by doing so they may look "stupid" or as if they lack knowledge. That is so far from the truth. How can anyone learn if they don't ask questions? Not one person on the face of the Earth outgrows learning. So, plunge that mentality right now! Learn to ask questions and, more importantly, be an avid listener. Also, realize that you can contribute to a conversation as well. Sometimes, you may feel your status or title does not allow you to have input, but remember that your life's experiences in the business world coupled with your personal life allow you to provide great objective feedback; use it when appropriate to do so. You never know how your input can benefit someone else.

Make sure that you are clear and direct in your communications.

Lack of confidence can come from feelings that others may not understand your message. Well, that's something you can fix. It's not always necessary to say or write a lot when you need to communicate your message. What is more important is that your message is presented with clarity and is direct and to the point. In this hectic world we live in, professionals are looking for less flowery messaging and more direct and to-the-point messaging. It helps others to see that you respect their time.

Question yourself less; you are intelligent.

Do you suffer from the feeling that maybe you are not smart enough in others' eyes? Well, you can squash that as well! No need to second-guess yourself. Many times, the people you are approaching regarding the product or service you offer know much less about it than you do and are looking to you as the expert. So step into that role. Remember that you are in the job because someone believed in your abilities. It's time for you to fulfill them. If, for some reason, you may not have an answer for someone, there is nothing wrong with advising them that you will research it for them and return with an answer. People respect your honesty, and they don't expect you to always have all the answers.

Be less defensive and more open to receiving constructive criticism.

In fact, ask for it. There is no need to feel threatened when others need to provide you with feedback to help you grow. Welcome it. Many times, it is difficult enough for the person providing it to have the courage to approach you when they see areas you can strengthen. Making it a great experience for them to do so helps them feel you are open to their feedback and to making necessary adjustments, or at least hearing them out. If you haven't had constructive criticism and you are unsure about your performance in a certain area, why not ask for it from someone you know that has your best interest at heart? This is another way of showing and gaining confidence in yourself. It will allow you an opportunity to fine-tune your abilities.

Flush It

Repeat your positive affirmation and complete the following exercise.

No longer will I be bound to this mind clogger, for it increases my anxiety and decreases my productivity! It is holding me back from my professional success. I am now free and walking with clarity because I have released it and flushed it down the drain! I am now unclogged!

Contemplate It

Let's complete your "flushing" by completing the following exercise.

I have identified the seed of my lack of confidence as:

I will take the following steps to flush this "clogger" so that I can be the best version of ME:

1

2

3

4

5

Rita Garnto

Simple Self-Care by Rita
Coach and Speaker

Tell us a little about your career background.

I became a registered respiratory therapist right out of high school, and that career spanned twenty years, allowing me to work in several different countries, including Canada, where I was born, Saudi Arabia, and here in the United States. This was an amazing career, and it allowed me to be a part of a team to help heal the young, old, and everyone in between. I even had the honor of being part of the trauma flight team at the Carolinas Medical Center for several years and flew on helicopters and airplanes transporting very sick patients.

As I neared the age of forty, I was getting burned out on the sickness, death, and dying working in the hospital and made the move to change careers to a more holistic approach. I went to school to become a licensed massage therapist while working full time as a respiratory therapist. Wanting to do things "my way," I opened my own private massage office shortly after retiring from my respiratory therapy career. In 2018, I closed my massage office after fifteen years and officially retired from massage therapy.

Becoming an author was the next adventure in my life journey. My book *Simple Self-Care Saved Me!* was released in 2018 and has sold copies in the US, Canada, Australia, the UK, and Europe and supports my passion for helping others to obtain better health and quality of life. My role now as a simple-self-care expert and stress management educator gives me a platform to help busy women and men stay ahead of stress burnout using very simple techniques discovered throughout my own very stressful life experiences.

When you evaluate your professional journey, what would you identify as your greatest mindset clogger?

Surprisingly enough, my self-confidence. It has taken me a long time to find my voice and be confident. I grew up not having an opinion of my own and having most of my decisions made for me. That created a lot of self-doubt and lack of self-worth. I also think part of the problem was that I did not always surround myself with the right supportive, loving people, and this caused a lot of second-guessing on my part. I am a bit of a visionary, and I think the people around me did not "get me" and my ideas or really understand where I was coming from, so it was easy to make fun of me and/or dismiss me. It is so much easier to doubt yourself and do nothing than to push ahead through the fear of possible rejection. I know that I am right where I am supposed to be, but I can see where along the way I could have moved up higher into management positions if I had more self-confidence and belief in myself.

What did you do to overcome it?

First of all, believing in myself was the first step, which was and still is a process. Second, I am very thankful that I am stubborn enough to keep trying to make tomorrow a better day, even if it takes me a week or a month to accomplish it. Yes, I am good at procrastinating and self-doubting. I use journaling, prayer, positive affirmations, creative visualization, exercise, and self-reflection to help get rid of the confidence negativity swirling in my brain. Yes, I use self-care and simple self-care to keep moving forward. I practice what I preach. Doing self-care and making time for just me helps me hear the whispers of God to help find my way, overcoming my self-confidence obstacles (and other obstacles as well). And thirdly, having a good support system filled with people who deserve to be a part of your story because they love you for who you are, with no hidden agendas, is the key. It truly takes a village, and you cannot do it alone.

What advice would you give to those struggling in this area?

Work on self-belief through positive affirmations such as "I love and approve of myself!" or "Yes, I can with ease!" or create one of your own. There are lots of good resources out there.

Look at yourself in the mirror, stare into your eyes, and declare your self-worth over and over again. Gaining self-confidence is a process and needs to be repeated over and over and over ... get the idea? It is not an easy win, but it can be done. Accept that you will have good days and bad days for the rest of your life. You will have days of great confidence as you forge ahead and also have days of self-doubt where you may stumble or take a step or two backward.

Surround yourself with people who believe in you and are not afraid to encourage and support you. Pick the ones who see the raw diamond deep inside and truly want to see you shine. These people will appear in your life, and you need to be on the lookout for them as they may not always be the most obvious. Believe and trust in yourself. Own your space in this world.

My successes include writing my book and being able to tell my story, being asked to be on the board of directors of a fabulous nonprofit foundation (thank you, Monique), and being able to forge ahead with my vision of making a difference in our crazy stressed-out world with my concept of simple self-care. I see all of my career choices as accomplishments and steps in my journey to self-discovery of self-confidence. I know this journey will never truly end. It is all about failing—failing fast, failing often, learning something from each failure, and adding that knowledge to your self-confidence armor to keep moving forward. I love and approve of myself!

Connect with Rita: Rita@SimpleSelfcare.net

Enjoy the Clear Passage

When you master confidence and raise your self-esteem bar, you will fare well. Just remember that I am speaking about confidence and not arrogance. The idea is developing a healthy level of confidence in yourself and your abilities to be successful, but never at the point of undermining others to make yourself appear "bigger." The simple adage "believe in yourself" says it all. When you have plunged and flushed this clogger away, the clarity in your capabilities and strengths will sparkle and shine in your own eyes and, by default, in the eyes of others.

MINDSET CLOGGER #4

Fear of Success

Just maybe you will be the next phenomenon. Oh wait! How will that happen if you are afraid to make a move?

Examine the Stoppage

You may be wondering, is "fear of success" really a thing? Could I really be afraid to be successful? Doesn't everyone desire a successful life? How in the world could I ever fear it? If these thoughts rolled through your mind when you heard this topic, you are normal. Isn't that a relief?! It really is hard to imagine how this is possible. Well, let me put it into perspective for you.

Have you ever been so close to a goal that you could taste it, and then you did some form of sabotage that stopped you dead in your tracks from completing it? What does that look like? Well, let's see—you were on a deadline, but a coworker wanted to go out for a drink, and you dropped everything to do that. You made a commitment that could make a major impact on your life, and you allowed some personal matter in your life to take precedent. You were so close to making a life-changing business decision, and cold feet caused you to say no without exploring all options. These are signs that fear of success may be stopping you from moving to the next level. So, let's get unclogged!

Plunge It

Fear of success is real! Identifying that it is holding you back is the first step in overcoming it. Here are a few tips that will begin the process of helping you diminish fear of success.

Focus On What Success Can Bring to Your Life

You may fear that once you become successful you won't be able to keep up with it. Plunge that concept! Instead, focus on what success will be able to bring to your life. Let's look at four benefits to success in your life.

You will gain greater confidence. Success is an achievement. When you reach it, because of your hard work and effort, you feel a sense of satisfaction from understanding what it took for you to get to that point. This gives you confidence and helps you gain a greater appreciation because you are now able to share the journey with others because you are a living, breathing testimony to the fact that success is achievable!

You will increase your network. To reach a level of success, you will have built meaningful relationships. A strong network is instrumental in gaining higher levels of success. The Rolodex of contacts that will open up as others grow to trust you and the quality of your goods and/or services is astounding. Plunge this fear so that you can grow into seeking out the relationships that will foster your success.

Your financial status will become less bleak. Achieving success results in a more solid financial status. When your financial status has significantly improved, more options are available for you to benefit your household and be a blessing in the lives of others in need.

Authenticity

You may fear the thought of becoming someone else. Don't think, "It may change me." Reflect on the value it will add to your life and, if applicable, your family. Focus on the additional time you would have to spend with family. Don't compromise your authenticity by trying to be someone you are not.

Big-Picture Thinking

Achieving success helps you understand that this is not about you. You will look back and see that achieving success has placed you in a position to see that you have become an inspiration to others. It provides you an opportunity to mentor others who look up to you as an example of someone who has overcome a fear of success. Small mindedness and selfishness will not have held you back, for you would have stayed focused on the lives of those you could impact positively through your example of achieving success, and that was the greater perspective.

Education

Success requires that you constantly educate yourself. You may feel that you cannot be successful because you can't manage all questions that may be

raised by others. This does not mean college degrees
or doctorates. Education comes from research and
looking for opportunities to gain knowledge. Mentors,
coaches, and experts in various fields are willing to help
you develop in the areas you are lacking. Once you
address the fear of success from this angle, you can
move forward.

Flush It

Repeat your positive affirmation and
complete the following exercise.

*No longer will I be bound to this mind
clogger, for it increases my anxiety and decreases my
productivity! It is holding me back from my professional
success. I am now free and walking with clarity because I
have released it and flushed it down the drain! I am
now unclogged!*

Contemplate It

Let's complete your "flushing" by
completing the following exercise.

I have identified the reason for my fear of success:

1

2

3

4

5

Shell Richardson

Owner
Elegant Connexions

Tell us a little about your career background.

I have always loved making people happy. When moving to Charlotte in 2005, I wondered what industry I would enjoy working in that could fulfill this love I had for serving others. Through Goodwill's Hospitality and Tourism program, I landed in the hotel industry for eight years.

My greatest mindset clogger was finding something I loved doing that would help others, yet wouldn't deplete me of my joy or energy.

What did you do to overcome it?

To overcome this challenge, I decided to become an entrepreneur by starting my own business.

What advice would you give to those struggling in this area?

I would encourage anyone struggling in this area to allow themselves the space and time to get to know what fuels them. What is something that you have always wanted to do? Is there something that sparks your interest but you don't know how to get started? Then I would encourage them to research that business. Find others who already have that business or a business and interview them about the good and the not-so-good of owning that business. This way, you have some practical information to go on.

**What successes have you achieved as
a direct result of plunging this clogger?**

I have now been an entrepreneur for seven years. It is hands down one of the best decisions I have ever made. I have grown so much as a person. The things that I used to worry about don't frighten me anymore. I understand now how to develop the process for what I want to do, then create the systems needed to execute my goals. I would encourage anyone to take the plunge. Start small and build as you go. One day, you will look back and see how far you have come, only to realize how much further you have to go. The difference, however, will be the understanding of how amazing the journey has been thus far. At that point, you will look forward to what is to come. The dream has started to become a reality. How exciting! I know it has been for me.

Connect with Shell: www.elegantconnexions.com

Enjoy the Clear Passage

A fear of success can paralyze you. Now that you have identified this "clogger," work really hard to overcome it. Do not allow small thinking, lack of knowledge, a small network, financial woes, or any host of outside mind corrupters to stop you from achieving success!

"Stay positive. Stay motivated. Stay encouraged. Most of all, believe in yourself and your abilities. After all, you can't expect people to believe in you and the services you provide if you don't believe in yourself."

MINDSET CLOGGER #5

Comparison to Others

Remember that no two people are alike. Value your uniqueness and stop wasting your time trying to be a clone!

Examine the Stoppage

Comparing ourselves to others is a natural behavioral pattern of humans. We tend to set bars, parameters, gauges, and limits on ourselves based on what we see others doing. Now, observing dangerous outcomes as a result of a particular path and ceasing that activity can make sense and would be a course of wisdom. What can become unwise and exhausting, however, is focusing so much on what others are doing that we become stagnant in our own success. It can cause us to second-guess our abilities. Or without us knowing all of the facts, we may assume reasons why someone is accomplishing something and pattern our actions after them. But our actions are unwarranted because they are working within a completely different set of parameters that we are not even aware of. This behavior becomes detrimental to our ability to prosper. So, if you have identified this as one of your cloggers to business success, let's get "unclogged."

Plunge It

Not comparing yourself to others can be a very difficult habit to break. Some have been doing it all their lives, and it results in a lack of joy, a decrease in self-confidence, and an extreme amount of anxiety. It also creates a fear of moving forward with meeting both personal and professional goals. So let's identify how you can turn around this pattern.

Pay Attention to Your Thoughts

The first step in working on an issue is becoming aware that it's actually a problem. You must become conscious each time these thoughts creep into your mind. Most of the time, you are comparing subconsciously, so start focusing on how often you are having these thoughts. By keeping a focus on them, you will start to realize how often you have them and will get in the habit of dismissing them.

Focus on Your Strengths

You must begin to realize that if others tried to compare themselves to your strengths, they would be exhausted too. So why not celebrate all of the "good stuff" you have going on? Be proud of your amazing qualities and what makes you unique. There is no need to boast, but you certainly deserve to use your strengths to your best advantage.

Realize Perfection Is Impossible

A part of why you may compare yourself to others is because you may feel you fall short in some areas. Well, you can relax in knowing that no one is perfect. You must learn to accept that and be OK with it. We all want to make improvements, but your quirks are what make you the unique individual or company that you are, so embrace it.

Don't Undermine Others

As a result of comparing yourself to others, you may feel inclined to be critical of them so that you can feel better about yourself. Refrain from this practice. You will only alienate others from you, and not only that, but also you will feel bad about yourself for doing it. Worst of all, you may snap a line to someone who could have been an ally in the future. Try to support others in their success journey. In the end, it will result in more success for you.

Focus Forward

Where you rank in comparison to others is really not important. You have your own journey, and it is not in competition with anyone else. It's yours and only yours. So, the only focus you should have is your journey to find, become, learn, or create something. No one else has anything to do with that, so focus on your task at hand and make every effort to complete it.

Flush It

Repeat your positive affirmation and complete the following exercise.

No longer will I be bound to this mind clogger, for it increases my anxiety and decreases my productivity! It is holding me back from my professional success. I am now free and walking with clarity because I have released it and flushed it down the drain! I am now unclogged!

Contemplate It

Let's complete your "flushing" by completing the following exercise.

Write why you are determined to break the comparison habit:

____

____

____

____

____

List your top five strengths that you will choose to focus on instead of comparing yourself to others:

1

____

2

____

3

____

4

____

5

____

Nesha Pai

Founder and Managing Member
Pai CPA, PLLC

Tell us a little about your career background.

I graduated magna cum laude from North Carolina State University and have held my CPA license since 1996 after passing my first attempt at the exam as a senior still pursuing my studies. I began my career and cultivated a passion for business planning within the world-renowned accounting firm Arthur Andersen and later within multiple, privately held Fortune 500 companies as a business consultant, relationship facilitator, and accounting analyst. I realized I had a passion for the small business and entrepreneurial sector.

Since starting my own firm in 2011, I continued nourishing my passion and the business growth of the Queen City by creating Pai Networking Group in 2017 and launching a podcast series, *Piece of the Pai*, that focuses on allowing successful entrepreneurs to share their business insight.

When you evaluate your professional journey, what would you identify as your greatest mindset clogger?

Caring about what anyone else thinks (the ones that don't matter, which is everyone outside of your inner circle) and the fear of failing. We cannot give power to anyone else because God has placed in each of us our unique destiny and dreams. Also, fear can be crippling. But if you have faith, the fear eventually diminishes.

What did you do to overcome it?

I had no choice but to overcome my fear of caring what others thought. I was a single mom with a mortgage and had to survive. I had walked out of my job with a boss who told me I would never be where my peers were because I was behind as a stay-at-home mom for six years in my career journey. That actually fueled me, and I am grateful we had that altercation that day, because I walked out and never looked back. I have had older male peers actually question or look down at my niche, but eight years later I am still here and moving upward.

What advice would you give to those struggling in this area?

Believe in yourself first and foremost. If you don't believe in yourself, you will ultimately fail. You are the driving force behind everything that you do. It takes confidence to go after your dreams.

I have built a firm with three stay-at-home moms working on my team, a podcast series, a networking group, and I published my book, *Overcoming Extraordinary Obstacles: Boldly Claiming the Facets of an Extraordinary Life.*

Connect with Nesha: www.paicpapllc.com

Enjoy the Clear Passage

Comparing yourself to others is detrimental to your ability to move forward. It's an unhealthy habit that takes time to undo, but you can if you focus on it. When you stay channeled, with your blinders on, you will enjoy your own journey that much more.

"Believe in yourself first
and foremost. If you don't
believe in yourself, you
will ultimately fail."

MINDSET CLOGGER #6

Stuck in Your Ways

They say you can't teach an old dog new tricks. I say, if the dog really wants to learn, he will!

Examine the Stoppage

If you know you are stuck in your ways and you find it extremely difficult to embrace change, you are not alone. You join others who have the same disposition for a number of reasons. First, it may just be your personality type. The DiSC method of analyzing personality types says a high C (conscientious and compliant) personality type tends to hold on to what they know and will not budge. You may happen to be such a personality type, and if so, if things are not "by the book," you find it difficult to consider anything else. Secondly, you may just be a mature person who feels you've lived on this earth long enough and don't need to budge for anyone if you don't feel like it. Third, you may feel everything in the world is swirling so quickly ahead of you that you just don't feel the need to catch up. If you have identified yourself in any of the above, it's the beginning of unraveling your thought processes and unclogging you!

Plunge It

Staying stuck in your ways will not benefit your professional success. We are living in times when efficiency, innovation, and flexibility are necessary for growth. As difficult as it may be to change, staying stuck is no longer an option. Plunging this mindset is a necessity! Here is how you can face this clogger in order to open doors of possibility for your future success.

Be Open to New Experiences

Trying new things can actually be more exciting than you can imagine. Start with small adjustments just for the sake of it. Try a new color, a new food, or a new way to get to work, or adjust some things on your desk or in your office and see how you like it. Learn to change things up a little. Even if you don't like it, you will realize nothing life-threatening happens when you adjust your norm. In fact, you may find it's much more fun than you expected. Go on—live a little while getting used to the idea of change.

Be Open to New Perspectives

You must understand that your way is not the only way. Try listening to other perspectives. Don't just cut people off when they are stating a way of handling a matter different from your customary way. Just because someone has an alternate perspective does not make them wrong; it's just another way to get the same job done. Try reading about different ways to accomplish the same tasks. You may be surprised to learn that there are more efficient ways to get the same job done and save yourself time and resources.

Honestly Evaluate Your Hesitations

Sometimes you may need to step back and ask yourself why you are so stuck in your ways. Is this more a matter of some hidden insecurities that you may have? If through an honest evaluation you identify that it is, work on the insecurities, and then change may become much easier for you.

Flush It

Repeat your positive affirmation and complete the following exercise.

No longer will I be bound to this mind clogger, for it increases my anxiety and decreases my productivity! It is holding me back from my professional success. I am now free and walking with clarity because I have released it and flushed it down the drain! I am now unclogged!

Contemplate It

Let's complete your "flushing" by completing the following exercise.

List three fears that you feel hinder you from change:

1

2

3

List the five benefits you know in your heart would come from getting "unstuck" in your ways and positively impact your professional success:

1

2

3

4

5

Kevin Douglas

CEO, Photographer, and Videographer
CapturedbyKevin

Tell us a little about your career background.

I am a veteran of the United States Air Force. After leaving the Air Force, I was picked up by NASA to work on the space shuttles' flight systems. By nature, I have a very technical skillset, so it is not surprising that I picked up the art of photography. I have been a professional photographer and videographer for over ten years, specializing in corporate photography. I have had the pleasure of working with numerous nationally and internationally recognized brands, such as Wells Fargo, Bank of America, Novant Health, Denny's,

YMCA, the AKA and Delta sororities, and Urban League, just to name a few.

When you evaluate your professional journey, what would you identify as your greatest mindset clogger?

Over the years, I realized I have hindered my business success by being stuck in my ways. I tend to get comfortable in a certain pattern, and once I am in that mode, it is difficult for me to shift.

What did you do to overcome it?

As my workload became greater, I realized the need to enlist the help of someone else in handling the administrative and marketing sides of my business. The need to scale my operation became a necessity to my business's growth and my development. It was no longer an option, but required, in order for me to be efficient and meet my clients' needs with a continued high standard of professionalism and excellence. I first sought the help of a business coach and then hired an executive assistant to handle the scheduling and marketing support that was needed. However, initially, taking my hands completely off the wheel and allowing her to handle the responsibilities I knew needed to be done was difficult. I eventually realized I had to trust her abilities and expertise, and I finally moved out of the way. When I did, my business began to flourish even more. My productivity and marketability were more effective, which resulted in increased profitability.

What advice would you give to those struggling in this area?

My advice would be to get out of your own way! Realize that your way is not the only way. Continuing in your old pattern, which is not producing your desired results, may require a change. Seek the advice necessary from a coach or mentor and do not be too proud to make necessary adjustments. Staying stuck in your ways will not contribute to growth.

What successes have you achieved as a direct result of plunging this clogger?

I have had the privilege of being one of the most sought-after photographers in the corporate space in my city and surrounding areas. My reputation for providing excellent service and quality work is what makes me stand out. I have won several awards and public recognition. I attribute all of this to my decision to let go of previous mindsets and be open to change. This has changed the trajectory of my business.

Connect with Kevin: cbkbrandingandconsulting@gmail.com.

Enjoy the Clear Passage

Unclogging your mind by understanding how being stuck in your ways hinders your progress, personally and professionally, will give you a whole new outlook! More importantly, you may be surprised to see how others will respond to you as they see you try to respect their viewpoints and input. You will see improvements in the systems around you as you embrace more efficient ways of conducting business. Who knows? A long-awaited position or financial increase may come as a result of the adjustment in your disposition because your boss may notice your ability to work with them and the team more effectively.

"Realize that your way is not the only way. Continuing in your old pattern, which is not producing your desired results, may require a change."

MINDSET CLOGGER #7

Technologically Challenged

When challenges present themselves, don't just throw in the towel. Find someone who can assist you in overcoming them. Sometimes you just need someone else to help you figure stuff out.

Examine the Stoppage

Being technologically challenged can certainly clog your mind and result in anxiety as you strive to professional success. Refusing to embrace technology will make your success even less likely. Technology now consumes almost every activity in our daily lives. For those who did not grow up with the level of technology that is utilized today, it can become a serious stumbling block to maneuvering through society. If you are struggling in this area, let's delve into how we can unclog this stoppage.

Plunge It

In order to plunge this mindset clogger, we must look at the benefits of technology. You must develop a determination to embrace it, get the help needed to learn how to effectively use it, and then develop the habits necessary to consistently integrate it into your professional life. Here are some tips to make embracing it less daunting.

Take It Slowly

You may now recognize the need to embrace technology, but don't feel you have to do it all at once. Pick which aspects need your immediate attention and begin there. Once you have mastered that one or those few, integrate what is necessary next. Technology is ever changing, so we all must take things step-by-step. It's much easier to handle when you take it in bite-sized pieces. Remember that you can't eat an elephant in one bite.

Seek Help

Most frustration comes in trying to figure it all out on your own. There is nothing wrong with accepting the fact that you may need assistance. If you need particular equipment, programs, or apps to improve your workflow, but you are struggling with installation or the most effective ways to utilize them, get the help that you need. Your company may already have a "tech department" that can assist. Use them! If not, take the time to find out if the brand you are using has a hotline or online chat available. You may need to look for online courses, books, or local classes that can assist you further. Do not let pride stop you from obtaining the help that you need to accomplish tasks more efficiertly. You will have a learning curve; however, just like riding a bike, once you get the knack of it, you will keep cruising.

Know When to Take a Break

You must realize that technology is helpful, but also realize it's OK to take a break from it when needed. You may find that you get frustrated in your attempt to learn how to work with your devices. In order to grasp the concepts, you may need to walk away from them for a while. Take a walk, get some fresh air, give your eyes a break, and then come back and try again. Even those who are technologically adept do the same at times.

Flush It

Repeat your positive affirmation and complete the following exercise.

No longer will I be bound to this mind clogger, for it increases my anxiety and decreases my productivity! It is holding me back from my professional success. I am now free and walking with clarity because I have released it and flushed it down the drain! I am now unclogged!

Contemplate It

Let's complete your "flushing" by completing the following exercise.

What are the top five systems, apps, or pieces of equipment that you need to upgrade in order to be more efficient?

(Research the cost and where they can be purchased, and list them in order of priority with an explanation as to how they will improve your professional success).

1

2

3

4

5

Interview with

Audra L. Hill

Speaker, Author, and Facilitator
From Trauma to Transformation: All Things New

Tell us a little about your career background.

For twenty-four years, I worked for Maryland state government as a claims specialist. Please know that this was a job I utterly detested. That was because I believed I was purposed and destined for something greater! With that strong conviction in mind, during a great deal of that same period, I was actively pursuing my dream of entrepreneurship by establishing my business as an independent beauty consultant with Mary Kay Cosmetics. Now, for almost the last four years, I have been honing my gifts as a preacher,

speaker, and teacher as a part of my purpose
and destiny.

When you evaluate your professional journey, what would you identify as your greatest mindset clogger?

I would identify my greatest mindset clogger to be
a fear of technology. More specifically, I had fear and
insecurity about learning and navigating through the
complexities of social media.

What did you do to overcome it?

To overcome that fear, I had to make a necessary
decision to "take the plunge" into the world of social
media using baby steps. I decided to launch out into
the deep of the unknown and discover where this
particular journey could potentially lead me.

What advice would you give to those struggling in this area?

The advice I would give to anyone struggling in
this area, would be to just do it. Please do not let
the simplicity of those words allow you to miss their
profundity. After all, those same words have served
as the famed slogan and trademark for Nike since
1988. These words serve to provide motivation and
empowerment to persons who either read or hear
them spoken. And if you desire to overcome your fear
of technology (macro level), and social media (micro
level), the only way to do so is to be resigned to just
doing it!

What successes have you achieved as a direct result of plunging this clogger?

Since resolving to plunge this clog of technological/
social media fear, I have grown a following of
persons who are being encouraged, enlightened,

and empowered by the content that I share. Equally as important, I am discovering and forging new relationships with leaders and supporters who are either assigned to inspire me, encourage, and cheer for me, and/or assist me with fulfilling my purpose and destiny. To that end, I am glad that I decided to overcome this fear. And because I believe the same opportunities and blessings await you, I encourage you to do the same. Overcome and prevail over the fear!

Connect with Audra: audrahill38@gmail.com

Enjoy the Clear Passage

Embracing technology is *huge*. Once you do, you will find that it was not as intimidating as you thought. I remember transitioning from one brand of phone to another and thought I could never make the adjustment, and now it's second nature. I figured it out. You will be so excited when you see the difference technology has made on your ability to connect with others for networking, to keep track of your time and appointments, to correspond more effectively with your customers, and to even be more time conscious in your travels. Removing this clogger will help free your mind once you get accustomed to it.

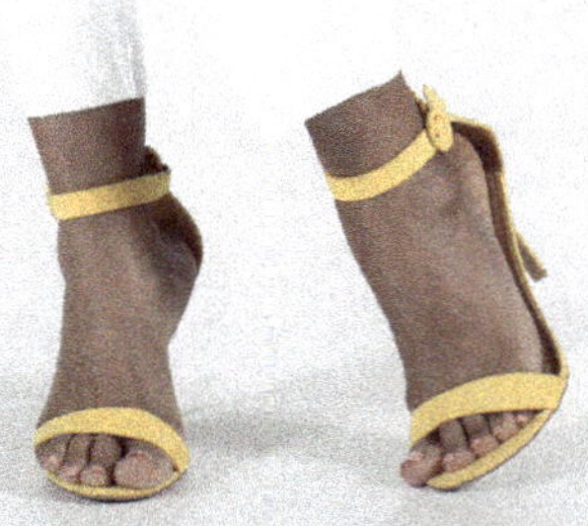

MINDSET CLOGGER #8

Disorganization

Cluttered surroundings clutter your thoughts and clutter your outcomes. Stop confusing yourself and everyone around you. Get organized!

Examine the Stoppage

Disorganization in your physical and mental space is damaging to your success. The first part of examining this stoppage is understanding why you are even dealing with it in the first place. Since acknowledgment is the first step to getting unclogged, circle items from the list below that may be your pain points, and then a little later we will cover why each of these are culprits to disorganization

- You think one huge list will settle it all.
- You were not taught how to organize.
- You are a procrastinator.

- You just have tons of stuff!
- Your timing is always off.
- You are the sticky note champion.

Plunge It

Disorganization is a challenge that cannot be corrected overnight. It's a tough one to tackle, but you can do it! It requires focus, systems, and determination. When you plunge this mindset clogger, it will seem as though life just became so much easier. You will move more freely, have fewer frustrations, and waste less time constantly looking for things. There will be a method to your madness!

As promised, let's break down reasons for disorganization and what simple adjustments can be made to help organize your life.

You Think One Huge List Will Settle It All

Talk about OVERWHELMING! Just imagine how long that list would be and how daunting on your mind it would be to try to get it finished. It's just like trying to move your home; would you put all of your belongings from every single drawer and cabinet into one HUGE box? Or would you have individual boxes that were specifically labeled for the room and/or drawer the items came out of? Certainly, the latter would be less confusing. So create different lists for specific items that need to be accomplished and categorize and organize these items. Smaller, more specific tasks and lists will help you check off faster and feel a sense of accomplishment as each list is accomplished.

You Were Not Taught How to Organize

We are creatures of habit, but if the habit was never developed, you have nothing in your reserve for you to behave differently. Now is the time to cultivate the proper habits. Set a new standard for yourself.

Come up with a system of organization that works for you and practice sticking to it. Learn how to move away from bad habits that keep you lazy and have become creative blocks to your getting the job done. (An example could be excessive television watching.) Find an accountability partner who can encourage you when you may be slacking to get back on track. Create an award system for yourself. With each series of tasks you complete, it helps getting organized a little more fun.

You Are a Procrastinator

Is "stall" your middle name? Do you find that every time you have a task to complete related to organization you become a master at finding other things to do, and somehow the task at hand does not get done? Maybe all of a sudden you need to hang some curtains or decorate the house. Maybe there's a Netflix movie you remembered you wanted to watch or maybe a surprise trip to the park is in order for the kids. These all become much more enjoyable things to do as opposed to completing what you really know needs to be done. Guess what? All of the above are great things to do, but those can be rewards once you have accomplished an organization task.

You Just Have Tons of Stuff!

Did you know you can be on not just physical clutter overload but also information overload?

Too much stuff everywhere! Clutter in your home, clutter in your car, clutter in your email, clutter on your social media platforms...clutter. Clutter everywhere.

Take the time to cleanse everything and learn to work with less. Have you heard of minimalists? They streamline their wardrobes, housewares, and decor. They have mastered living with less and testify to the fact that their lives are so much simpler with less.

Your Timing Is Always Off

Do you feel like you are always late, never prepared, and when you finally show up you are feeling frazzled? That's a sign of a lack of organization when it comes to your time. Making the comment "oh, I'm always late," gets old. At some point, it would behoove you to address it and make some changes.

Start by setting a timer on yourself to make it a point to arrive ten to fifteen minutes ahead of time. Instead of waiting until the hot last second to get out of bed when you know you have an appointment, develop a new morning routine that allows you sufficient time to calmly get dressed, without the adrenaline rush, from your poor timing. Now here's a tip that's revolutionary: you can really go that extra mile by laying out your outfit the night before. Imagine the time you will save by not rummaging through your closet and drawers, which adds to clutter as you toss everything in them out, if you would reduce one less step that will stress you out and make you late every time.

You Are the Sticky Note Champion

Loose paper and little sticky notes are probably your friends. You want to talk about huge distractions to developing a sense of organization?! Using this as a method of remembering what you need to get done is counterproductive. These little pieces of paper will become such a pain to deal with. As they pile up, you will see that it adds to clutter, and you may lose some of them with the "great notes" you had on them to keep you straight.

A better solution is to have one journal or notebook where you house all notes that need to be made. This can more readily travel with you. Also consider embracing technology by using the "notes" section of your phone or even creating your lists on your computer. Find out what will work best for you and your lifestyle, and then toss those sticky notes and reduce clutter and frustration in your life.

Flush It

Repeat your positive affirmation and complete the following exercise.

No longer will I be bound to this mind clogger, for it increases my anxiety and decreases my productivity! It is holding me back from my professional success. I am now free and walking with clarity because I have released it and flushed it down the drain! I am now unclogged!

Contemplate It

Let's complete your "flushing" by completing the following exercise.

List up to five culprits to your disorganization from the list above in the order you plan on working to organize them in your professional life:

1

____

2

____

3

____

4

____

5

____

LaGuida Moore

CEO, LaGuida Moore Photography
Photographer and Graphic Designer
BalloonPOP, Balloon Design Artist

Tell us a little about your career background.

I have a criminal justice degree but fell in love with photography. I caught the "I want to try modeling" thing while in college, and from there my love of photography grew, while learning the industry of modeling. From there I learned a lot about lighting and techniques, posing, movement, equipment, and gained a better understanding of what it takes to stay and make it just a little in the industry. But again, I became more interested in the technical part and the why, how, and what. And so I said, "I want to learn that and understand photography and take beautiful photos and be a professional photographer!" So after my first daughter was born, I had a model! I did an apprenticeship with a local photographer, learned studio and a lot more, and continued to connect with other professionals, workshops, seminars, and attended conferences. I went crazy practicing on her and family members, and I have not looked back, and I love every minute!

Now, along with being a photographer I became a stay-at-home mom for the next twenty-plus years. And photography was, of course, a huge part of my identity. BalloonPOP and decor came along much later, and I fell in love with it as well! I got introduced to it by being in the right place and being curious and asking a lot of questions. But my dear friend took the time to show me and explain the process and allowed me to work alongside her in Atlanta for different events. She told me I could do it, so I decided to give it a try. I've been growing slowly and at a nice pace.

When you evaluate your professional journey, what would you identify as your greatest mindset clogger?

Disorganization with my mind, my schedule, and my business operations. I like being able to follow through on a sale and not reduce my price for service and product. Next, being able to walk away from a client if it does not benefit my time and talent.

What did you do to overcome it?

Creating systems for myself and getting organized has helped tremendously. Getting organized for me consisted of getting a coach, getting an accounting service, and saying no to people. It's better time management. Also, rebranding myself and setting that expectation along with a better experience for a great outcome for my client and myself.

What advice would you give to those struggling in this area?

Get help and know that you may need guidance and someone who can hold you accountable. Set your price. Know what you want to make, have that number set, and make it happen! Know your worth and value for your skill set and market. Have great customer service—connect with your clients!

What successes have you achieved as a direct result of plunging this clogger?

Having the confidence to know my value as a photographer, knowing my worth, and enjoying the clientele that values my services. I have accepted the need to change to move forward with the use of technology, increased my educational skills, growth, and lastly, I rebranded myself.

Connect with LaGuida: laguidamfoto@yahoo.com

Enjoy the Clear Passage

Disorganization makes you feel as though you are getting nothing accomplished. Getting to the root of your disorganization, and dealing with solutions to it will allow the fix to be permanent. You will have changed the habits that result in the chronic disorganization. You may work on improving this mind clogger on your own, but don't be afraid to call in a professional organizer and/or a coach who specializes in this area to really make sure you have cleared this passage well.

MINDSET CLOGGER #9

Distorted View of Money

Detach your happiness from what's in your bank account. Money can come and go. A rich lifestyle has nothing to do with money and everything to do with mindset.

Examine the Stoppage

This mindset clogger is a game-changer if corrected. In our personal and professional success, how we view and handle our finances can be the difference between a financial demise and a comfortable lifestyle. If you know that controlling your finances is the struggle that is hindering your success, then you need to pay keen attention to how to turn around your mindset and channel your thoughts in the right direction. I certainly have had times when my view of money became distorted. I truly believe that as you go through different stages in your life you may formulate poor habits connected to money in order to protect your level of anxiety or to serve as a distraction from the reality of your current situation.

Here are some poor habits to watch out for identified by author Kevin Voight in "7 Bad Financial Habits You Need to Break Right Now" of the NerdWallet.[3] See if you are practicing any of them.

- Spending more than you earn.
- Ignoring your bills.
- Thinking more cash brings happiness.

Plunge It

A distorted view of money can impact you in so many ways. Usually, your habits have been acquired through your upbringing or your personal life's journey. Know that whether you learned these habits early or late in life, they are just that—habits, which means they can be broken if they are poor. One thing is for sure if you are practicing any of the poor habits listed above: you must break them before you go broke, if you haven't already. So let's go back to a few poor habits that the personal finance writer of NerdWallet has to share regarding why these habits must be plunged.

Stop Spending More Than You Earn

"About one in five Americans spend more than they earn, and 38 percent break even…Your goal must be to join the 40 percent of Americans who spend less than they earn." (Voight 2017). Credit cards are a great culprit for this. Credit cards can literally become an addiction

---

3. Kevin Voight, "7 Bad Financial Habits You Need to Break Right Now," Nerdwallet (blog), March 17, 2017, https://www.nerdwallet.com/article/finance/9-financial-bad-habits-stop-money-problems.

if you are not careful. They can become a trap to keep you indebted. You have to remember that there is a price for their use. The more you spend, the more you must pay back. If you know you don't have the financial resources or savvy to pay them properly, it's best not to use them until you develop a level of discipline.

Another culprit that expands upon this habit is the ATM. Just because the cash machine keeps letting you withdraw from it, that doesn't mean you should. One of the worst habits is to never look at your account balance before you withdraw from an ATM. It's one of the fastest ways to bankrupt your household. The overdraft fees can pile up, and next thing you know your entire next paycheck will be sucked into the hole you have created. It's a vicious cycle that you don't want to get caught up in. If you are already a culprit, now's the time to stop it! So whether you're using a credit card or a withdrawal from the ATM, make sure you have the cash first before you make the purchase! You are not the "fifth regiment," so stop charging!

Stop Ignoring Your Bills

Some people only pay the bills when the collection agency calls. According to Voight, "this kind of financial firefighting only guarantees you'll veer from crisis to crisis as your credit score burns. Payment history carries huge weight on your financial future; more than one-third of your credit score is judged by your ability to pay your power bill, car insurance, and credit cards on time." (Voight 2017). He also suggests working out a payment plan with your creditor before it goes to collections.

When I was a single parent with three small children and operating on a shoestring budget, I developed unhealthy money habits. First, I began not opening the envelopes with bills as they came in the mail. Somehow, I had convinced myself that if I didn't look at them, they did not exist. The problem with that is, after a while, that thought process will create more stress. Bills begin to pile up, and then they move into collections; this increases mail, unwanted phone calls, and, in turn, increases stress levels, which clogs you up!

Now I've learned that facing bills head-on reduces anxiety. Even if I can't pay it immediately, I know I can call and communicate with the creditor. Most will allow you to schedule a later payment or even a payment arrangement. What I learned was that communication is the key.

I no longer let the bills pile up. I open them, schedule them out, and take joy in paying them on time. If a "life ooops" happens, I know a phone call to the creditor works.

Stop Thinking More Cash Brings Happiness

They say that "money can't buy you happiness," but it can...up until a point.

So, let's put this in total perspective. Money can buy you things that can add joy to your life. Material things such as nicer homes, cars, fine clothing and great vacations are a plus. Money can even allow you to be in a position to bless others and that is definitely something beautiful. However, you cannot view money as your true source of happiness. The thing that makes money an unreliable source of happiness is today you may have plenty, and in a blink of an eye it could be gone or diminished to a point you could have never anticipated. Stock market crashes, pandemics, loss of jobs, and even sickness can result in money diminishing without warning and can change the trajectory of your life.

Happiness comes from within you. If you learn to tie your happiness to a sense of contentment with yourself first, you will realize that no matter how much money is in your bank account, you can be happy. People have found in times of financial devastation that healthy relationships with others, developing a sense of faith, enjoying the beauty in nature, and spending time with supportive family and friends have all brought much joy. For these things have nothing to do with money, they are the real sources of happiness. Developing an appreciation for what really matters will help you understand why I always say "being rich has nothing to do with money but everything to do with mindset."

Flush It

Repeat your positive affirmation and complete the following exercise.

No longer will I be bound to this mind clogger, for it increases my anxiety and decreases my productivity! It is holding me back from my professional success. I am now free and walking with clarity because I have released it and flushed it down the drain! I am now unclogged!

Contemplate It

Let's complete your "flushing" by completing the following exercise.

List the top three financial habits you've identified you must break ASAP in order to grow professionally:

1 ______________________________________

2 ______________________________________

3 ______________________________________

Interview with

Francene Marie Morris

Radio Personality,
Beasley Media Group
Founder, Speaker, and Coach of
My New Strut

Tell us a little about your career background.

My broadcast radio journey began in 1996 after a public speaking and modeling agency career. My everyday adventure consists of hosting and producing syndicated talk-radio programs for various stations that include top 40, country, hip-hop, R&B, adult contemporary, rock, and sports.

My greatest mindset clogger was the notion that men were the only ones back in 1996 making a name for themselves in radio, with the salaries to match. But I soon realized I'm one of the most creative minds producing informative talk shows in the Southeast region. Having to carve out my own path in broadcasting is the best ongoing project to date.

What did you do to overcome it?

I overcame that debilitating mindset after my personal life crashed and burned, coupled with a layoff. I knew I had to quickly walk into the light and see all of my talent as a plus or allow the self-saboteur to control my existence.

What advice would you give to those struggling in this area?

It's OK to talk to yourself! Pump yourself up with compliments. You are the total package with room for exploration. In the morning, say to yourself, "Job well done!" before you start out of the gate. Since life dishes out stages, phases, and changes at any given moment, remember all the struggles and frustrations in your professional life offer a choice to hinder or grow you.

What successes have you achieved as a result of plunging this clogger?

I've enjoyed working alongside the Charlotte Symphony Orchestra, working for just about every media outlet, and winning radio personality awards. Creating *Good Mood Workshops* and *My New Strut* workshops for women with a desire to put a pep in their step is also rewarding.

Connect with Francene: mynewstrut@gmail.com

Enjoy the Clear Passage

When you substitute your poor financial habits with good ones, that's progress. By replacing your unproductive financial routines with great financial habits, you will understand what financial freedom looks like. When finances are in order, you will improve your bottom-line revenue. Bills must be paid in a timely manner. Technology will help you manage and maintain your financial future.

MINDSET CLOGGER #10

Image Insecurities

Feeling confident about your exterior is an interior job.

Examine the Stoppage

Do you find yourself hesitant about networking or representing your company or brand in the public eye because you feel your personal presentation is lacking the professionalism you would like others to see? Well, this section is for you. Adjusting your mindset is the first step in overcoming this clogger. If you look in the mirror and what you see makes you feel insecure, then fixing it is as simple as deciding to do it.

Plunge It

Below are some common thoughts that may hold you back from addressing your professional presentation. Circle all that apply to you.

- I'm not confident enough to correct my image. I wouldn't know where to begin!
- Shouldn't I wait until I lose weight to go on that journey?
- No one else around me cares, so why should I?
- I don't want people to think I've changed and then start treating me differently.
- It's going to cost too much money to revamp my image!

Let's review each of these concerns so that, once and for all, you can plunge this clogger down the drain!

Sometimes we may not have the expertise to correct our own image. This is where you may need to get help. You can go to a good friend or family member who you know is well put together and ask them to assist you. If no one in your circle seems appropriate, your local department stores may have stylists available who can lead you in the right direction. If you feel you would like more personalized assistance, you may hire a personal stylist in your area to work with you one-on-one; many will go shopping with you or shop for you in order to take the stress off your mind. Whichever avenue you choose, realize you do not have to do it alone.

Losing weight before you choose to address your professional image does not make sense. No matter what size you are, there are professional, complimentary styles available. You must take pride in yourself first. Your coworkers and clients still deserve to see you look your best. Learn to have confidence in yourself no matter your weight. The mindset should be that no matter what size you wear, if your clothing fits appropriately and is stylish, you deserve to step out and feel your best!

The choices of your workmates should not dictate how you carry yourself. You may feel inclined to follow the crowd in relaxing your look, but if in the back of your mind you do not feel comfortable in doing so, don't do it. Remember that maintaining a standard of excellence in your professional presentation, despite what the crowd is doing, will help you stand out. Behind the scenes, both employers and human resources comment on the employees whose image is impeccable. When it comes time for promotions or special opportunities to represent their brand, those who show they care about their own presentation will tend to receive those opportunities first. Your image certainly does matter.

At times, a fear of standing out from the rest or appearing as though you think you are better than everyone else may cause you to hold yourself back. You must remember that anyone who faults you for looking your best has their own insecurities to deal with. You cannot take those on. If your desire is to move up and demonstrate you have leadership potential, or if you are already in a leadership role and want to maintain the respect of your team, you cannot afford not to pay attention to your image. If no one else in the office cares, you set the pace for them to step up.

Today, spending an enormous amount of money on clothing is not necessary. Having a few quality pieces that are interchangeable keeps your wardrobe simple and affordable. Thrift stores and consignment shops now make it possible to purchase quality, even high-end name brands, at a fraction of the cost of what you would spend in the department stores. Dressing for less is now becoming the norm. Once again, seek help from someone who can assist you in where to shop in your area within your budget.

So now that we have cleared up these misconceptions, let's move along to getting unstopped in this area.

Flush It

Repeat your positive affirmation and complete the following exercise.

No longer will I be bound to this mind clogger, for it increases my anxiety and decreases my productivity! It is holding me back from my professional success. I am now free and walking with clarity because I have released it and flushed it down the drain! I am now unclogged!

Contemplate It

Let's complete your "flushing" by completing the following exercise.

Make a list of at least three individuals in your circle whose professional style you admire.
Write their names and phone numbers down. I encourage you to go ahead and pick up the phone and reach out to them. Explain that you love the way they coordinate their look and that you are looking for assistance or even a few pointers on how you can level up your image in the workplace. You will be surprised at

how willing they will be to help. If you do not have such connections in your circle, contact three local department stores and ask whether they have stylists available. If they do, schedule an appointment to have someone work with you on creating a signature look that is complementary to your size and personality. You can also ask around for recommendations for personal stylists within your community whom you can hire to be of assistance. Either way, you must start somewhere, and putting pen to paper with suggestions begins the process.

1

____

2

____

3

____

Interview with

Nora D. Richardson
CEO and Owner
Spot-On Branding LLC

Tell us a little about your career background.

For the past twenty years, I have been fixing brands for companies and entrepreneurs. Companies come to me when their branding and marketing isn't generating leads. I come up with strategies that align the prospect's perception to their expectations.

When you evaluate your professional journey, what would you identify as your greatest mindset clogger?

My greatest mindset clogger was when I decided to get on stage to speak about branding. My company brand was on point. My personal brand needed to match. I had nice clothing but not stage-worthy clothing. I was everyday presentable. But everyday presentable isn't stage presentable. This is a problem for anyone who wants to present on stage but especially for a branding expert. It stopped me in my tracks.

What did you do to overcome it?

I needed to figure out how I wanted to be perceived. Like in branding companies, I knew my audience was going to judge me by my appearance. I needed to create a look and feel in my wardrobe that reflected who I was, so they could instantly resonate with me on stage. I didn't want my clothes to be a distraction but to enhance who I am. I knew I wanted a fun but timeless look … more classic than vintage. I loved the '40s and '50s polka dots, and that went well with my company brand name, Spot-On Branding. I figured out I needed help achieving the overall look.

So I hired people. I had to. I needed to know what cut of clothing enhanced my physical attributes. I also needed to know how to put on makeup. I am more of a natural, "come as I am" kind of gal, so the last time I really put on makeup, blue eyeliner, blue mascara, and blue eye shadow was the trend. Gotta love the '80s.

I hired a style coach to help me find the right clothes that fit and give me the brand look that differentiates me from other speakers and other branding experts. I hired a makeup artist to show me step-by-step how to achieve a flawless but natural look and then how to adjust the look for the stage. Lighting can be so harsh.

What advice would you give to those struggling in this area?

If you are struggling in this area, I would suggest asking for help. When you can, hire experts. Know that when you invest in yourself, others will invest in you. In this case, I knew branding. I knew what to do but not how to achieve the look I desired. I could have figured it out eventually, but by hiring people, I instantly came on the speaking scene looking like a professional. People instantly treated me as an expert in my field. I looked and felt like a million dollars, which only added to my confidence and others' confidence in me.

What successes have you achieved as a direct result of plunging this clogger?

I have spoken to international and national audiences, I have made speaking a profitable part of my business model, and I average fourteen speaking gigs a year, which is just the perfect amount for me. Plus, I have clients all over the world.

Connect with Nora: www.Spot-OnBranding.com

Enjoy the Clear Passage

Understanding the need for establishing a strong professional presence through your image and communication is important to your professional success. It makes a clear statement that you take pride in yourself and the brand you represent. More importantly, it will build your self-confidence because you know that you are putting your best foot forward to maintain a standard of excellence. And that is the strongest statement of all!

"I knew what to do but not how to achieve the look I desired. I could have figured it out eventually, but by hiring people, I instantly came on the speaking scene looking like a professional."

THE CONCLUSION OF
THE MATTER

Thank you for taking the time to read this book, *Unclogged*. I do hope that you have taken the time to use the exercises in this book to delve deeper into how you can become a more successful professional. I also hope that you were able to identify specific areas where you feel you are "clogged" in your professional success and that you have meditated on how you can unstop, flush, and plunge away the things that are holding you back. The processes may not be easy, and it may take time and practice. I know that if you continue to press forward, you will overcome, and you will be able to reach your goal for your business.

Obtaining knowledge is not something that we want to hold to ourselves. The best way that we can be of benefit to each other, and help each other grow, is to share information. So please take the time and pass on this book to someone else whom you feel can benefit from the information enclosed. Help someone else to become unclogged in their professional success, and in so doing, we all rise together.

A part of our growth is also allowing ourselves to be vulnerable, which is very difficult for many of us as human nature does not allow us, at times, to feel comfortable expressing areas where we may be weak. In order to grow, however, we must be vulnerable sometimes. It is not a sign of weakness; it is a sign of strength. It shows we are willing to expose the areas where we need help, and when we express this to others who are in a position to assist us, we cannot help but grow.

Now that you have identified the areas where you feel you need help, seek out mentors and individuals who have been through some of the very situations you have expressed in writing in the exercises. As you complete your exercises, take time to sit with your mentors to ask questions and to learn how they, in their life's journey, were able to overcome the things that had them clogged. You will be surprised how many people share similar circumstances as you. But they won't know that you could use help from their stories if you don't open up and share areas in which they can help you.

I look forward to hearing about your success as a result of applying what you have learned in this book. Wishing you continued professional success on your business and personal life's journey.

Monique Douglas

**"Unclog your mind, for less
stress means more success."**

-Victoria Hall, Monique's
thirteen-year-old daughter

BIBLIOGRAPHY

Hill, Napoleon. *Think and Grow Rich.* The Ralston
   Society, 1937.
Voight, Kevin. "7 Bad Financial Habits You
   Need to Break Right Now". *The NerdWallet.*
   March 17, 2017. Accessed November
   2020. https://www.nerdwallet.com/article/finance/
   9-financial-bad-habits-stop-money-problems.
Washington, Denzel. *A Hand to Guide Me.*
   Meredith Books, 2006.

ACKNOWLEDGMENT

Mike Knoble

CEO
Silky Shea by Mike

Mike, you have the ability to juggle a progressive body care product company while holding down a full-time job as well as having the responsibilities of being a husband to your supportive wife and a parent. It was a pleasure to work with you as your coach during a time when you felt "clogged" with regards to direction and effective systems to take your company to the next level. It is a blessing to see you implement your action plan in conjunction with your vision and mission for your brand.

You have effectively developed independent contractors to represent your brand in multiple states. You have repackaged your products to an upgraded look and feel in harmony with the direction of your brand. You are a fine example of a leader who guides through your own example of work ethic and stellar customer service.

I am looking forward to seeing your brand grow globally! You are truly an example of an entrepreneur who was willing to invest in your own personal and professional development. You made the investment worthwhile by making application of what you learned, and then sharing the knowledge with those you lead.

For this reason, I am excited to showcase you in this published work. In your case, clarity certainly delivered results.

Learn more about Mike's brand: www.SilkyShea.com

ABOUT THE AUTHOR

Being great means being an "outsideboxer." That's who Monique Douglas is! She is a native of Nassau, Bahamas and a resident of Charlotte, North Carolina. Her fresh approach to life is a result of her belief that "despite life's ups and downs we must take time to enjoy life's journey, because happiness truly is a choice!" Her life's motto is to "Stop ... Smell the roses ... Pick one ... And pass it on." She is dedicated to a life of serving others professionally and through community service.

Monique is a business consultant, keynote speaker, author, and poet. Her goal is to uncover potential from within and then groom those whom she has the privilege of working with to greatness.

As former CEO of Clear Communication Consulting, she is now a partner with her husband, Kevin Douglas, in CBK Branding & Consulting Firm LLP and enjoys identifying ways to help professionals understand the connection between their personal and business professional brands. She enjoys curating clear, dynamic, and consistent messaging surrounding her client's personal brands to help them make a "splash" in the marketplace.

Monique has over thirty years in cosmetic and
hospitality sales and management. She has led teams
to over half a million dollars in annual sales continually.
Maintaining a standard of excellence in hospitality,
leadership, and community service has resulted in
numerous awards, including her induction in 2018
into the Women's History Hall of Fame at the Levine
Museum of the New South in Charlotte, North Carolina.

She currently serves on the Board of Directors
and is the director of community engagement for The
Brooklyn Collective.

As a result of her commitment to youth and their
families, Monique founded the Grooming Greatness
Foundation in 2014, a non-profit organization non-profit
focused on bonding parents, guardians, mentors, and
their youth through the grooming process. The goal
of the foundation is to groom them into well-rounded
productive members of society as they educate,
enrich, and expose them to the endless possibilities for
their future success.

Engaging with Monique results in you walking away
refreshed and invigorated as a result of her positive
mindset and genuine love for people.

Her favorite quote, which of course she penned,
is, "A rich lifestyle has nothing to do with money but
everything to do with mindset."

"A rich lifestyle has nothing to
do with money but everything
to do with mindset."

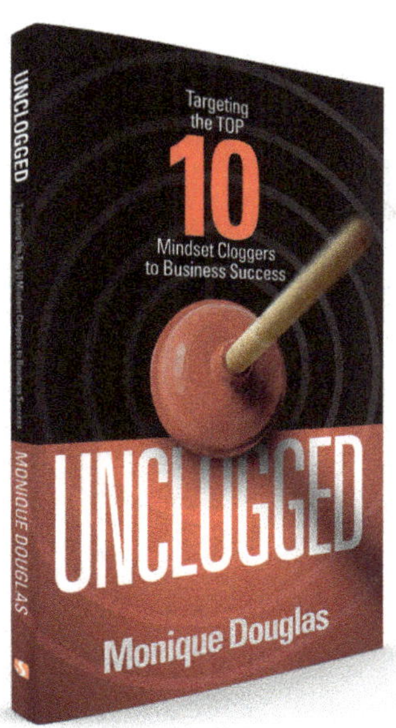

Contact Us

CBK BRANDING AND CONSULTING

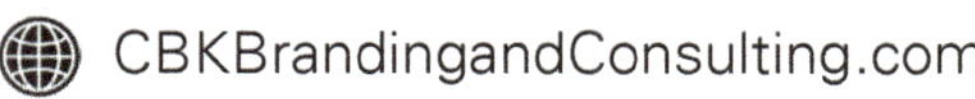 CBKBrandingandConsulting.com

 cbkbrandingandconsulting@gmail.com

GROOMING GREATNESS FOUNDATION

 GroomingGreatness.org

 Monique@GroomingGreatness.org

Printed in the USA
CPSIA information can be obtained
at www.ICGtesting.com
CBHW052112290824
13875CB00032B/189